It's Okay

Written and Illustrated by:
Maya N. Johnson

Copyright © 2020 by Maya N. Johnson

All rights reserved. No part of this book may be reproduced or used in any manner without written permission of the copyright owner except for the use of quotations in a book review. For more information, address: mnbortters@gmail.com

www.mayanjohnson.com

To all of the love and support I receive.

It is a bright and sunny Monday. Little seven-year-old Ivy is eating lunch and talking to her mommy and daddy about all of the fun things she loves to do.

"Mommy! Daddy! I love to play outside and go swimming. I love to paint pictures of animals and bake yummy cookies. I also love to read and learn about science," Ivy says as she is enjoying her lunch.

Ivy's mommy looks over at Ivy with a warm smile and says, "Those activities sound like they are a lot of fun to do!"

The next day Ivy wakes up feeling sad. Before she jumps out of her bed, Ivy begins to think about why she does not have the same joy about doing her favorite activities that she loves to do.

As Ivy is sitting and thinking in her bedroom, she hears her mom yell, "Ivy, it is time for breakfast!"

At the breakfast table, Ivy's parents notice that she is not feeling cheery and happy.

Feeling concerned, Ivy's daddy asks, "Why is my pretty daughter feeling down today?"

"I do not know, daddy," Ivy answers.

"Hey, I have an idea! Let's go to the store so we can buy food to bake cookies. You love to bake yummy cookies," Ivy's mommy suggests.

Sadly, looking down at her breakfast, Ivy replies, "No, mommy. I do not enjoy to bake cookies anymore.

Ivy's mommy says, "That's alright, honey. I have another idea! Let's go out and get some ice cream to try and cheer you up."

Ivy replies, "Okay, mommy. Ice cream sounds yummy."

Ivy has a tiny smile on her beautiful face, but she feels like she is going to start crying. She wants to talk to her parents about how she is feeling but feels really scared.

After Ivy and her mommy return home, Ivy goes into her bedroom to think.

Ivy wants to know why she is feeling down about enjoying all of the fun activities she loves to do. Ivy also wants to know why she does not enjoy smiling anymore.

As Ivy thinks in her bedroom, she begins to cry.

Ivy's mommy and daddy hear her crying in her bedroom. They walk up to her bedroom and check on her to see if she is feeling okay.

Feeling worried, mommy says, "Ivy, mommy and daddy are here to talk to you about how you are feeling."

Ivy's daddy adds, "Mommy and I see that you are not feeling happy. Why is our beautiful princess crying?"

"I do not know, daddy," Ivy answers as she begins to cry harder.

"It's okay, sweetheart. You can always come to mommy and daddy to talk about how you are feeling and what you are thinking," Ivy's mommy says as she wipes the tears off of Ivy's face.

Feeling more comfortable, Ivy explains, "Okay, mommy. I have been feeling really sad and down about everything. I do not feel happy about the fun activities I love to do. I get scared when I try to think about how I feel. I want to be happy, but I feel stuck."

Ivy's parents begin to cry as they look at each other. They both give Ivy a big hug and a kiss on her forehead.

"Oh, Ivy! Mommy and daddy are sorry that you are feeling down. We are both here for you and always will be. It's okay to have these thoughts and to feel afraid. Mommy feels afraid sometimes, too," Ivy's mommy answers.

Ivy's daddy adds, "That's right, honey. We want to help you understand all of your feelings and thoughts."

Feeling a little better, Ivy asks her parents, "How?"

Thinking, Ivy's mommy says, "Let's make a feelings chart. We will draw five faces: one for happy, one for silly, one for angry, one for afraid, and one for sad. Every morning you can pick a face, and that will let us know how you are feeling. After you pick a face, daddy and I will sit down with you and talk about the face you picked. Let's call them feeling faces!"

Ivy's parents see that her smile is growing bigger. They smile with her and hold her hands.

Ivy says, "I love your idea, mommy."

Ivy's daddy adds, "Me too!"

"We want you to know that it's okay to talk about how you are feeling. It's okay to feel scared, and it's okay to cry. We want to help you face your feelings because our brave little girl can take on the world," Ivy's parents answer as they embrace her.

"My sweet, beautiful princess, daddy often felt really sad when I was a little boy. I was really afraid to talk to my mommy and daddy about how I felt. They taught me a phrase to help me: it's okay. They helped daddy learn how to talk about how I felt when I didn't feel happy," Ivy's daddy says as he is comforting her.

"I didn't know that other people can feel sad, too. I thought it was only me. Now I know it is okay to talk about how you are feeling when you don't feel happy," Ivy states.

"My sweet girl. Of course, it is okay to feel down. It's okay to come to mommy and daddy when it is hard to understand how you are feeling. You can always come to us when you need to talk about what makes you feel sad," Ivy's mommy says warmly.

Ivy's daddy proudly adds, "You are our smart and funny daughter who is very gifted. Mommy and I want you to always remember: It's Okay."

Feeling warm inside, Ivy repeats, "It's okay to talk about how I feel. It's okay to feel down. It's okay not always knowing how to understand my thoughts. It's okay to ask mommy and daddy for help. It's Okay!"

Ivy gives her parents the biggest hug and kiss she has ever given.

Ivy excitedly yells, "Thank you mommy and daddy! Can we all say our phrase together?!"

"Of course, honey!" her parents say.

"It's Okay!" they all scream together.

As they all are sitting on Ivy's bed, Ivy turns to her parents and happily says, "I love you mommy, and I love you daddy!"

Ivy's parents reply, "We love you, our beautiful and talented daughter! Everything is going to be okay."

After that day Ivy slowly becomes happier and happier. Everyday Ivy wakes up, picks a feeling face, and talks to her parents about the face she picked and how she is feeling. She then recites the phrase her parents taught her: It's Okay.

The end

CPSIA information can be obtained
at www.ICGtesting.com
Printed in the USA
LVHW020830171120
671904LV00010B/463